STAGECOACH IN SCOTLAND

THE FIRST TWENTY YEARS

KEITH A. JENKINSON

AMBERLEY

First published 2018

Amberley Publishing
The Hill, Stroud
Gloucestershire, GL5 4EP

www.amberley-books.com

Copyright © Keith A. Jenkinson, 2018

ISBN 978 1 4456 7871 9 (print)
ISBN 978 1 4456 7872 6 (ebook)

British Library Cataloguing in Publication Data.
A catalogue record for this book is available from
the British Library.

Origination by Amberley Publishing.
Printed in the UK.

Introduction

Born as a family business in Scotland in 1980 and originally operated as GT Coaches with a solitary vehicle, Stagecoach quickly grew and today has a global fleet of around 10,400 buses and coaches, approximately 8,200 of which are operated in the UK, with 1,400 of these being in Scotland. Never afraid to experiment or introduce new concepts in public transport, Stagecoach gained its first local bus operations south of the Scottish border in April 1987 as a result of the sale of the NBC. The company then gradually expanded its operations across large parts of Britain, as will be shown in a forthcoming volume. Although this book only traces the company's developments in Scotland between 1980 and 1999, following the start of the new millennium it has continued its growth across the country and this will be detailed in a future publication.

Without the help of others, and Campbell Morrison in particular, for allowing me to use their excellent photographs, there would have been numerous gaps in the pictorial content, and thus to all those who have assisted I offer my sincere thanks. The photographs that are uncredited are from my own camera, while those whose names are unfortunately unknown to me are shown as Author's collection. To the latter I apologise profusely and hope that they will forgive me for using their work, but will nevertheless enjoy seeing it in print, as their contribution is greatly appreciated.

Keith A. Jenkinson
Queensbury,
Bradford
2018

Stagecoach in Scotland 1980–1999

The history of Stagecoach dates back to 1976 when Ann Gloag and her husband Robin began a small self-drive motor caravan rental business under the title of Gloagtrotter from their home in Perth. As the venture grew, they diversified into self-drive minibuses and then in March 1980 purchased a Deansgate-bodied Ford Transit minibus, which they operated as GT Coaches on private hire duties. Shortly before this diversification they were joined by Ann's younger brother, Brian Souter, and upon learning of a party who intended making an overland trip to China, purchased their first full-sized bus – a second-hand ex-Bristol Omnibus Co. forty-five-seat ECW-bodied Bristol MW5G – to enable them to quote for it. Unfortunately, the China trip never materialised and instead a contract was gained to transport workers employed on a road scheme between Perth and Pitlochry. As a result the bus's £425 purchase price was recouped within weeks and, filled with enthusiasm, a former National Travel West Alexander-bodied Leyland Leopard was bought to expand the private hire operation, this then being followed by an ECW-bodied Bristol MW6G and a five-year-old Duple-bodied Volvo B58.

Meanwhile, upon learning of the new Transport Act, which allowed operators to run express services of over 30 miles without the need for the customary authorisation, GT Coaches took the decision to introduce a four times weekly overnight service from Dundee to London. Using the title 'The Stage Coach', this commenced on 9 October 1980 using the Volvo B58 and a recently acquired second-hand Plaxton-bodied AEC Reliance, the fare being £9.50 single, which cut that charged by the Scottish Bus Group by £2. While the success of this new operation led the company to extend this route to Aberdeen from 26 January 1981, prior to that it had gained a foothold in local bus operation when on 22 December 1980 it purchased the Perth to Errol service from McLennan of Spittlefield. Although the latter's Errol depot was included in the deal, none of its buses were, which resulted in four second-hand Bristol Lodekkas being purchased – three ex-Central SMT FLF6Gs and a convertible open-top ex-Bristol Omnibus Co. FS6G – all of which were repainted into GT livery.

In March 1981, GT Coaches purchased its first brand-new vehicle, a Duple Dominant III-bodied Volvo B58, which it painted in a white livery with red, blue and gold stripes together with the new Stagecoach fleet name. With passenger numbers on its Anglo-Scottish express services continuing to grow, during the following year it was found necessary to obtain some larger coaches, and to this end, with financial assistance from Ann and Brian's uncle, Fraser McColl, two new double-deck Neoplan Skyliners were purchased, followed by an ECW-bodied Bristol VRLLH6L that had begun life with Standerwick. The latter, however, proved unreliable and was sold after only six months, whereas the Neoplans were excellent and a further six were acquired in 1983, along with three Van Hool Astromegas. Six more Bristol FLF6G Lodekkas were also added to the fleet during the same year.

Always innovative, on 22 June 1983 Stagecoach introduced a programme of day tours under its new 'Fantasia Tours' banner from Crieff, Perth and Dundee to places such as the Trossachs and Loch Lomond, upon which it employed its Neoplans and Van Hool Astromegas and served lunch and tea onboard, both of which were included in the ticket price. Then, seeking to expand even further, on 29 August 1983 Stagecoach began a new express service between Waverley Bridge, Edinburgh and Park's City coach station, Glasgow, with twelve journeys in each direction seven days each week. With a fare of £1.30 single, which was lower than that charged by the Scottish Bus Group, with whom it competed, it also offered a continental breakfast en route for a further 40p. Requiring a base in Glasgow from which to maintain its new service, it leased a small depot/workshop close to the city centre at North Canal Bank Street, Port Dundas. This was not all, however, as on 11 November 1983 it purchased Edinburgh coach operator Adamson & Low to give it a foothold in a new area, and although its seventeen coaches were included in the deal, most were quickly replaced by newly acquired second-hand vehicles (including two ex-Leicester City Transport MCCW-bodied Leyland PD3s) and some coaches transferred from Perth. Quickly following this, Stagecoach took over the operation of Park's of Hamilton's Glasgow to London service, although on this occasion no vehicles were involved; instead, Park's continued to provide them and fitted them with removable Stagecoach name boards.

Such was Stagecoach's rapid expansion that by the end of 1983 its fleet had grown to sixty-one vehicles, of which forty-seven had been added since the start of the year. In addition, for several months the company hired a Duple-bodied and two Caetano-bodied Volvo B58s from Whyte of Newmachar and repainted them in its corporate colours. Before the year ended, however, and following a breakup of his marriage, Robin Gloag left the Stagecoach partnership in December and set up a business on his own under the title of Highwayman Coaches, initially from Stagecoach's Friarton Road, Perth, premises before moving to Errol during the early part of 1984.

After the events of 1983, the year that followed proved to be comparatively quiet except for the company's move from Friarton Road to a new base at Walnut Grove, Perth, in August 1984. A former car showroom, this provided spacious office accommodation, a well-equipped workshop and a large parking area for the expanding fleet and thus placed everything on one site for the first time. This in turn allowed the former McLennan Nissen hut depot at Errol to be closed and sold, with its small vehicle allocation being easily accommodated at Walnut Grove.

In contrast to the previous one, 1985 proved to be a year of many changes, the first of which took place in January when Stagecoach surprisingly purchased five Routemasters from London Buses, these being the first of their type to operate north of the border, or indeed outside of London except for those purchased new by Northern General. After initially remaining in store at Walnut Grove, the first of this quintet was placed in service in March, still in its former operator's red livery, on the service from Perth to Errol. Then, by the time the others had made their debut, a further five had been purchased (in May) and gradually all began to be repainted into Stagecoach's corporate colours. In the meantime, following increased competition from the Scottish Bus Group, the express service between Edinburgh and Glasgow was discontinued from 10 March and the depot at Port Dundas was closed. With further plans obviously in mind, however, its lease was retained, and as will be seen later, it was ultimately brought back into use.

Despite having enjoyed a period of rapid expansion, its Adamson & Low operation in Edinburgh had not measured up to its expectations and in May it was placed in voluntary liquidation and closed. Immediately following this move, the business and three coaches were re-purchased by G. Adamson, one of its original owners, while the remainder of the Edinburgh fleet was returned to Perth. Then, proving that expansion was still clearly on Stagecoach's mind, on 11 November it purchased the whole of the assets and operations of old established Spittalfield-based A. & C. McLennan to give it numerous local bus services and contracts to the north of Perth. Included in the deal were twenty-six buses and coaches, of which nine were double-deckers, and although some of these continued to be operated by Stagecoach, none lasted long enough to be repainted into their new owner's colours, with their replacements being quickly sourced.

With the deregulation of local bus services looming on the horizon as a consequence of the 1985 Transport Act, Stagecoach, like many other operators across Britain, began to look at ways in which it could use the new legislation to its advantage. The ability to be able to operate services without being blocked by other operators led the company to register three services in Glasgow, and for this purpose it formed a new company under the title 'Magicbus (Scotland) Ltd' – the registered office of which was its depot at North Canal Street, Port Dundas. Starting its new operations to East Kilbride, Castlemilk and Easterhouse on D-Day, 26 October, the latter of these ran on an express basis via the M8 motorway to provide a speedy service between this large housing development and Glasgow city centre. The fleet transferred from Perth to Glasgow for the new Magicbus operation comprised fourteen Routemasters (including three recently acquired front-entrance examples that had begun life with Northern General), two Bristol Lodekkas and five Volvo B58 coaches, all of which carried Magicbus fleet names. In addition, following the failure of Scottish Bus Group subsidiary Strathtay Scottish to register its Perth to Pitlochry and Pitlochry to Aberfeldy services for continuation after 26 October, Stagecoach took them both over to further consolidate its position in this area.

After a period of comparative calm, Stagecoach ventured forth again in 1987, when it bought a further twenty-four Routemasters for its growing Magicbus operation in Glasgow. Twelve came in November from group subsidiary Hampshire Bus, where they had remained unused since their purchase from London in May, nine were bought direct from London Buses and the other four were front-entrance examples that had started life with Northern General or British European Airways.

Also joining the Magicbus fleet between November and February 1988 were ten Van Hool McArdle-bodied Ailsa B55s that had been new to South Yorkshire PTE but had latterly been operated by Stagecoach Hampshire Bus, with four then being loaned to Stagecoach Cumberland before reaching Glasgow. All retained their Hampshire Bus livery but, never proving popular, were all withdrawn by the end of May and dispatched to Spittalfield to await their disposal later in the year. Some of these replaced the original Routemasters, which were also placed in store at Spittalfield, some never to operate again while others were later returned to service. Meanwhile, on 12 October Stagecoach purchased Glasgow-based Cotters Coachline express services together with eight Van Hool-bodied Volvo B10Ms and its spacious depot at Warroch Street, to where the Magicbus fleet was transferred, thus allowing the company to vacate its Port Dundas base.

More surprising, however, was the purchase between October and December of no fewer than thirty-four Alexander-bodied Leyland Leopards from Scottish Bus Group subsidiary Kelvin Scottish. All were taken to Spittalfield for storage, with only fourteen of them being placed in service by their new owner, the remainder either being cannibalised for spares or ultimately sold to other operators. Even more surprising, however, was the purchase of a former McLennan Leyland PS1, which was acquired for preservation by the company but also made occasional appearances in service after being fully restored and repainted into its original livery. Also in the news was Stagecoach's first brand-new coach, Volvo B58 FES 831W, which was returned to Duple to have its body rebuilt to Dominant II specification and fitted with fifty-nine bus seats, after which sister JSR 42X was similarly treated, but retained its coach seats.

While 1988 proved to be a quiet year, on 1 May Stagecoach unexpectedly purchased Glasgow-based McGill's two ex-South Yorkshire PTE Leyland-DAB bendibuses. It intended to use these buses on its Magicbus services, but after some deliberation sent them instead to Hampshire Bus, who placed them in service around Winchester. Then, in November a Bristol VRT was borrowed from Stagecoach Cumberland to trial it in Perth as a possible successor to the Bristol Lodekka; finding it successful, it was joined in January 1989 by four similar buses acquired from Devon General, with a further four from the same source joining them in May.

Venturing forth again on the acquisition trail, Stagecoach purchased Highwayman Coaches and its five vehicles from Robin Gloag in February 1989, although its depot was not included in the deal, this being retained for his new body repair business with Stagecoach guaranteeing a one-year contract to undertake work on its growing fleet. Meanwhile, amidst great secrecy Stagecoach was plotting an attack on Scottish Bus Group subsidiary Strathtay Scottish, and for this purpose began to amass a number of Leyland Nationals from its English subsidiaries – Hampshire Bus, United Counties, Cumberland and East Midlands. While seven of them were placed in service in Glasgow by Magicbus in May, the remaining fifteen were held in store at Spittalfield to await further developments. Following the creation of a new company, Perth & District Buses Ltd, this came on 19 June when they appeared bearing Perth Panther fleet names on two new cross-city services in Perth that shadowed Strathtay's most lucrative routes. These were joined by a third service on 17 July and soon afterwards by one from Perth to Pitcairngreen, the latter being maintained by Stagecoach Volvos and Leyland Leopards which were also adorned with Perth Panther fleet names. With the gloves now off, Strathtay responded by repainting six of its Routemasters into a new red and cream livery with Perth City Transport fleet names, reminding the city's residents of the W. Alexander days when its Perth operations used that colour scheme.

Having taken the decision to give total concentration to its bus operations in Scotland and England, on 4 August Stagecoach sold its entire Perth-based long distance coaching activities together with its Walnut Grove base and thirty-one coaches to National Express who, for its purchase, formed a new company, Tayside Travel Services Ltd, which was to trade under the identity 'Caledonian Express'. As part of the sale agreement, Stagecoach allowed its name to continue to be used on publicity material and its former coaches for a period of two years, and was granted permission to continue the use of Walnut Grove until an alternative depot and headquarters could be found. Before the month ended, new administrative accommodation was sourced in Charlotte Street in the heart of the city and then on 21 October Stagecoach opened a new depot on the fringe of the Inveralmond Trading Estate, Perth.

Meanwhile, the battle with Strathtay continued to rage when, on 21 August, Stagecoach moved northwards to Dundee where it began a competitive service from the city centre to Monifieth using six Leyland Nationals. It had been planned that these would use the fleet name 'Tay Tigers', but as this was already the identity of a locally based ice hockey team, it was decided instead to brand the vehicles with its established Stagecoach name. A week later a second service was started – to Carnoustie – and to save dead mileage to and from Perth arrangements were made for parking, etc. at the Dundee Depot of Greyhound Coaches. As a consequence of the introduction of services in Dundee and the ongoing battle in Perth, Stagecoach needed more buses, and to satisfy this purchased eight new Robin Hood-bodied Iveco 49.19 minibuses in July, additionally hiring twenty Ford Transits from Devon General in September. All the latter were surprisingly delivered by rail and retained their rightful owner's livery until their ultimate return in February/March 1990.

Turning its attention to expansion yet again, on 11 November 1989 Stagecoach acquired the business of Inverness Traction through its Magicbus subsidiary, taking it to an area of Scotland in which it had not previously operated other than with its express coach services. Included in the deal were twenty-two Freight Rover Sherpa minibuses and six Leyland Leopards, of which two of the latter had only been purchased from Stagecoach four months earlier. As all the minibuses had been leased, their new operator was keen to return them to their rightful owner as soon as possible and thus replacements were quickly drafted in from other Stagecoach companies to allow their release. Among these were ten ex-Zippy tri-axle Talbot Pullmans that had been in store with Stagecoach Cumberland, all of which still retained their yellow livery, some ECW-bodied Leyland Leopards from Cumberland, and two Leyland Nationals from Perth.

Over the next two years, in addition to a large number of new Iveco 49.10 and Alexander-bodied Mercedes-Benz 709D minibuses being purchased for use in Perth, Glasgow and Inverness, the flood of second-hand buses from Stagecoach's subsidiaries south of the border continued with numerous Bristol VRTs arriving as replacements for Routemasters and Lodekkas – two of the VRTs being ex-Southdown convertible open-toppers, which it put to use on its city tour. Also joining the Magicbus fleet in Glasgow in January 1990 were eight NCME-bodied Leyland Atlanteans, which had started life with Greater Manchester PTE but had latterly served with Stagecoach Ribble. Later, in October of that year, four Routemasters were put to use on Perth city services, where they were joined in June 1993 by a further three and remained in daily use until their final withdrawal in December 1996, becoming the last Routemasters to be operated by Stagecoach outside London. More noteworthy, however, was a brand-new 110-seat Alexander-bodied tri-axle Leyland Olympian, which entered service with Magicbus in April 1989 and carried 'Megabus – Britain's largest bus' lettering. In the meantime, on 25 February Magicbus had vacated its Warroch Street Depot in the heart of Glasgow and relocated to a new site at Hobden Street in the Springburn area of the city.

Having had its sights firmly set on the privatisation of the Scottish Bus Group, Stagecoach finally achieved its goal when it purchased Northern Scottish Omnibuses on 27 March 1991, thus extending its established Scottish network to the northern coast and adding another 206 vehicles to its growing empire. Almost immediately Stagecoach renamed the company Bluebird Buses and began a programme to repaint its buses into their new owner's corporate livery. Then, almost before the ink had dried on its new acquisition, it purchased the Aberdeen to Banchory service of Clark of Banchory together with three Leyland Leopards, all of which were quickly sold. Clark's Taxis & Coaches was not included in the deal, however, and continued independently from its existing premises at Dykehead Garage. In addition, during the autumn Stagecoach acquired the remaining Highland Scottish operations in Inverness and the Easter Ross area, adding a further thirty buses to its Inverness Traction fleet and giving it a depot at Tain.

Following its success in northern Scotland, Stagecoach was delighted to learn on 29 May that it had been named as preferred bidder for Scottish Bus Group subsidiary Fife Scottish. However, only hours before the announcement was made by the Scottish Office, a group of Central Fife Members of Parliament protested vigorously at the decision and demanded that reconsideration was given to a bid submitted by Fife Scottish's management and employees. As a result, the unusual decision was taken to allow the latter to submit a revised bid; this failed and on 23 July Stagecoach became the subsidiary's new owner. This added a further 300 buses and coaches along with seven depots to Stagecoach's Scottish operations and gave it control of the whole of the east of Scotland northwards from the River Forth.

Over the next three years, consolidation appeared to be the key north of the border. During this time Stagecoach made massive gains in Inverness from Highland Scottish, which required an additional thirty-six vehicles, and after gaining a number of tendered services from Strathtay Scottish in the Crieff area and the closure by Strathtay of its local depot, it opened a new outstation in the town. On the debit side, as a result of having its sights set on the acquisition of Strathclyde PTE's arms-length Strathclyde Buses (which in the event it failed to achieve), it sold its Glasgow Magicbus operation and depot to Kelvin Central Buses on 10 April 1992 to pave the way. The twenty-four buses involved in the deal included a number of Routemasters.

Then, on 11 May 1992 Stagecoach began a nightly rail service between Aberdeen and London after striking a deal with state-owned Inter-City, under which Stagecoach leased six railway carriages that it repainted into its corporate livery to become the first privately operated passenger train since the railways were nationalised in 1948. After a less than a happy ride, this venture ceased in October 1993 but had at least provided the company with some experience of rail operation. All this paled into insignificance, however, as on 27 April 1993 Stagecoach Holdings was floated on the London Stock Exchange with an issue price of £1.25 per share. Within minutes all the shares were taken up and over the next few weeks their value increased dramatically. Meanwhile, Stagecoach continued to expand its services in Perth, causing Strathtay to further retreat and close its depot in the city. Throughout this period new buses continued to arrive in quantity, with Mercedes-Benz 709Ds, Dennis Darts and Volvo B6s, B10Ms, and Olympians joining the Scottish subsidiaries who also saw older vehicles transferred between them or from the company's English subsidiaries, while the striped corporate livery continued to be applied at an increasing pace.

1994 saw Stagecoach on the acquisition trail once again when in January, through its Bluebird subsidiary, it purchased the eighteen-vehicle family owned Norrie of New Deer and during the following month the eleven-coach Hans Hardy of Aberchirder. While only three minis from Norrie's fleet were retained, all those acquired with Hardy's business continued in service with their new owner. These were small fry, however, compared to the purchase of former Scottish Bus Group subsidiary Western Scottish from its management and employee owners on 24 July. In addition to adding a further 340 buses and coaches to its empire, it introduced Stagecoach to a wide area of south-west Scotland and also provided it with several Scottish Citylink contracts. Then, almost before it had settled into its new area, its recently acquired subsidiary looked across the Firth of Clyde and on 1 October purchased the Isle of Arran twenty-four-vehicle operator Arran Transport & Trading Company who maintained a number of local bus services on that island, Bute and the Cowal peninsula. Its thirteen Bedfords, four Mercedes-Benz minis, a DAF coach, a Leyland Cub, three Leyland Nationals and a Dennis Dart all continued to operate for their new owner but were subsequently replaced by buses transferred from the Western Scottish fleet.

Having withdrawn from local bus operations in Glasgow in April 1992 and failed in its attempt to buy Strathclyde Buses, Stagecoach decided to start a new network of services in the city on 19 November 1994 using eighteen new Alexander PS-bodied Volvo B10Ms and planned to introduce more new services early in 1995 when the Glasgow fleet would expand to sixty buses. For this new operation it proposed purchasing Clydeside 2000's Thornliebank depot, but these plans never reached fruition as on 15 November, following an approach by the chairman of Strathclyde Buses, Stagecoach acquired a 21.7 per cent share in SB Holdings, which was the parent company of Strathclyde Buses and Kelvin Central Buses. This resulted in Stagecoach cancelling its plans to re-enter Glasgow and selling its new Volvo B10Ms to Kelvin Central Buses.

As 1994 ended on a high note, so 1995 began in similar fashion with Stagecoach purchasing the bus operations of A1 Service of Ardrossan on 29 January, an Ayrshire bus co-operative whose ten members all retained their individual premises while those who also ran coaches kept these too, although a large number of the seventy-five inherited buses remained in service with their new owner and retained their existing blue and cream livery, albeit with the addition of Stagecoach (A1 Service) fleet names. Moved to Stagecoach Western's Ardrossan depot, these were supplemented with several Bristol VRTs transferred from Stagecoach's English subsidiaries and a number of Leyland Titans from Stagecoach London, the latter at first retaining the red livery of their previous owner. Ultimately, however, under its new ownership A1 Service was maintained as a separate unit and retained its blue livery and fleet name until the twenty-first century, when it was replaced by Stagecoach corporate colours and identity. Later in the year A1 Service entered into a joint venture with Clyde Coast Services and AA Buses to operate a service branded 'Clydecoaster' between Ayr and Greenock, and later, on 4 September, acquired Clyde Coast Services' six local bus routes to leave that company to concentrate on the Clydecoaster service and a number of contracts. In the meantime, on 24 July A1 Service had taken over three services in the Irvine/Kilmarnock area which had been operated by Valley Bus Company prior to its licence being revoked. Then, before 1995 drew to a close, Stagecoach Bluebird purchased the twelve-vehicle Elgin-based Scotravel, although neither its taxi business nor depot were included in the deal.

Following the sale of Strathclyde Buses to First Group, on 3 June 1996 Stagecoach sold its 21.7 per cent stake in the company to its new owner while during the same month Bluebird was granted the 'Royal Warrant of Appointment to Her Majesty the Queen' as suppliers of bus and coach services between Aberdeen and Balmoral on the occasions of visits by the royal family. As a consequence, the royal coat of arms was applied to the company's Ballater depot vehicles. This was not all, however, as on 12 July Stagecoach Fife introduced two new high-floor Jonckheere-bodied Volvo B10M bendicoaches on its X27 express service between Anstruther and Glasgow. Seating seventy-two passengers, these 18-metre-long coaches were joined in August by two similar coaches from Stagecoach East Midlands, albeit with Plaxton bodywork. Finally, in October Bluebird purchased the six-coach business of J. S. Gordon of Dornoch, and although all its vehicles were included in the deal, none were operated by their new owner and were immediately sold.

Still having its sights on Glasgow, on 24 April 1997, from a new base at Cowcaddens, Stagecoach launched three new services in the south of the city to and beyond the Pollock Centre using twenty-six new dual-purpose-seated Alexander-bodied Volvo B6LEs. In addition, from the same date it began a half-hourly express service from Buchanan bus station to Cumbernauld which competed directly with Kelvin Central Buses, this being maintained by Fife's bendicoaches from its Dunfermline depot. These, however, were only phase one of Stagecoach's assault on Glasgow as on 12 May it introduced a new ten-minute frequency express service to Easterhouse and thirteen days later began two services to East Kilbride. For these operations it received eleven new Northern Counties-bodied Volvo B10Ms that had been diverted from an order intended for Stagecoach Manchester and sixteen Mercedes-Benz L608Ds transferred from Stagecoach Cumberland and Stagecoach Burnley & Pendle. With the Cowcaddens depot now being too small to house the growing fleet, a second depot was obtained on the Blochairn Industrial Estate alongside the M8 motorway. Still building on its successes in Glasgow, two more services were launched on 9 June (to Castlemilk) followed on 23 June with three services to Drunchapel and Milton. Meanwhile, on 16 June Stagecoach had struck a deal with Park's of Hamilton, who registered a local service in East Kilbride for which Stagecoach provided Mercedes-Benz L608Ds. Then, on 28 June the two services from Buchanan bus station to Newton Mearns were enhanced with twelve former London Leyland Titans transferred from Stagecoach Western, while on 21 July yet another new service started between Pollock Centre and Cardonald. With the arrival of some new Alexander PS-bodied Volvo B10Ms in August, the eleven Northern Counties-bodied examples were then able to be transferred to their intended Manchester owner.

Later in June, on the 29th, Stagecoach Western Scottish acquired Dodds of Troon's AA Buses local bus operations and forty-one buses, leaving Dodds to continue its coaching activities. As Dodds retained its depot, the AA Buses operation was moved to Stagecoach Western's Ayr depot from where it was maintained as a standalone unit retaining AA's green and cream livery and fleet name. Among the vehicles inherited in the deal was Dodds' preserved Burlingham Seagull-bodied Guy Warrior which was loaned to Stagecoach, who repainted into the old Bluebird livery and put it to use on its Heritage Tour of Perthshire from Edinburgh.

In October, Stagecoach Western Scottish repainted one of its ex-London Leyland Titans into an all-over yellow livery, upon which large 'School Bus' lettering was added, this being the prelude to several other buses being similarly treated. In addition, another of Western's ex-London Titans was given an overall promotional livery for a service from Ayr to the nearby Butlins holiday camp. Back in Glasgow, a tendered service between Parkhead and Cambuslang had been gained on the 19th.

Over the past few years, Stagecoach Fife had received a large number of Bristol VRTs cascaded from its English subsidiaries to maintain its large number of schools services, but as these buses were nearing the end of their expected lives, in November 1997 they began to be replaced by Leyland Titans previously operated by Stagecoach in London, which were converted from dual to single-door configuration before entering service in their new home.

Diversifying from its road transport interests, in 1996 Stagecoach surprisingly formed a new company, Stagecoach Aviation Ltd, which purchased Prestwick Airport in Ayrshire. Although the airport had lost most of its passenger traffic as a result of the expansion of Glasgow's air terminal, it had dramatically increased its freight activities and had gained some charter passenger work, with Stagecoach planning to gain more commercial passenger flights. Looking to expand in its new field, Stagecoach Aviation then submitted bids for the purchase of Skavsta Airport near Stockholm, Wellington Airport in New Zealand and Humberside Airport in England, but sadly none of these came to fruition.

After launching a Perth summertime hop-on, hop-off bus tour in 1997 using an open-top Bristol VRT, this was repeated from 2 May 1998, although on this occasion in conjunction with Guide Friday, and maintained by two of Bluebird's open-top ex-London Leyland Titans.

As it approached the new millennium, Stagecoach could look back at its growth in Scotland with a great deal of satisfaction, having grown from a single-vehicle coach operator into a company that provided bus and express coach services across a large part of the country. Throughout the 1990s Stagecoach had continued to upgrade its Scottish fleets with new Mercedes-Benz 709Ds, Dennis Darts, Volvo B6s, B10Ms and Olympians and had expanded its express service network with new coaches while its corporate livery now reigned supreme across Scotland. Looking ahead into the twenty-first century it would, however, gain an even greater share of the Scottish market as it purchased more bus operating companies, the story of which will hopefully be told in a future volume.

Standing in October 1980 at the London terminal of Stagecoach's new Anglo-Scottish service, for which it is branded, is Duple-bodied Volvo B58-56 LYS 457P which was new in September 1975 to Park's of Hamilton. (Author's collection)

Stagecoach Duple-bodied Volvo B58-61 HSP 593W stands alongside Excelsior of Bournemouth's Plaxton-bodied Ford R1114 PJT 518W and Abbeyways of Halifax's Plaxton-bodied Ford R1014 FCX 578W in the spartan surroundings of Kings Cross coach station, London, in July 1981.

Parked kerbside in Glasgow in 1981 wearing GT Coaches livery is ex-Western National ECW-bodied Bristol MW6G HDV 639E, which is now preserved by Stagecoach. (Author's collection)

The first Bristol FLF6G Lodekka to be purchased by GT Coaches (in January 1981) was former Central SMT FGM 306D, seen here in Perth in its new owner's original livery. Sadly it was withdrawn from service following an accident in September 1985 and was scrapped a few months later. (Author's collection)

The first vehicle to be purchased new by Stagecoach was Duple Dominant III-bodied Volvo B58-61 FES 831W which was first registered in February 1981. Here it is seen with its original body which was later rebuilt as a Duple Dominant II. (John Law)

Acquired from Bristol Omnibus Co. in April 1981, convertible open-top ECW-bodied Bristol FS6G 866 NHT is seen here still wearing GT Coaches livery but sporting a Stagecoach fleet name and an aircraft logo on its side panels. In 1990 it was transferred to Stagecoach Hampshire Bus and is today owned by East Yorkshire Motor Services. (P. McElroy)

Standing at Waverley Bridge, Edinburgh, ready to operate the express service to Glasgow on 27 September 1986 is Stagecoach Duple Dominant III-bodied Volvo B58-61 JSR 43X, which had been purchased new in November 1981.

The amusing name board above the doorway of the former GT Coaches Depot at Perth Harbour was still visible on 21 August 1989.

With lettering promoting Stagecoach's Perth to London service on its upper side panels, and painted in GT Coaches livery, ex-Central Scottish ECW-bodied Bristol FLF6G HGM 335E is now preserved by Stagecoach and kept at the Scottish Bus Museum at Lathalmond. (Author's collection)

The first of several Neoplan Skyliners to be purchased by Stagecoach, LSP 222X was bought new in May 1982 and is seen here wearing its owner's corporate livery with Super Stagecoach lettering. (Author's collection)

Parked alongside each other are Stagecoach's Van Hool Astromega TD824s NDS 842Y and NDS 841Y, both of which were new in March 1983 but had comparatively short lives with the company. (Author's collection)

Wearing the livery it carried when purchased new in June 1983 from a Limebourne, London, cancelled order, Neoplan Skyliner MVL 607Y carries a Stagecoach name board at the base of its windscreen and is seen here resting alongside Van Hool Astromega NDS 841Y. (Author's collection)

Adamson & Low's Plaxton-bodied Ford R192 OSG 741Y was rebuilt in September 1982 from Barrie of Balloch's NSN 888G which was new in March 1969 and also carried a Plaxton body. (Campbell Morrison)

Painted in Stagecoach corporate livery but operated by its Adamson & Law subsidiary, former Leicester City Transport MCCW-bodied Leyland PD3A/12 LJF 27F only spent a short life in the fleet, being purchased in January 1984 and sold twelve months later. (Campbell Morrison)

One of three coaches hired from Whyte, Newmacher, in 1983, Caetano-bodied Volvo B58-61 WCO 733V, which had begun life with Trathens of Yelverton in March 1980, is seen here in Park's City coach station, Glasgow, painted in Stagecoach corporate livery. (Author's collection)

Purchased by Stagecoach from Clyde Coast Services, whose livery it still carries, Plaxton-bodied Volvo B58-61 BGG 160S, seen here in Glasgow, had started life with Park's of Hamilton in May 1978. (Author's collection)

Surprisingly purchased by Stagecoach in August 1988, but sold three months later without being operated, was ECW-bodied Bristol K5G JVW 430 which was new to Eastern National in February 1944 and is now preserved. Here it is seen at the front of Stagecoach's head office and depot at Walnut Grove, Perth, on 29 August 1988.

Having just arrived at Spittalfield after its purchase by Stagecoach from London Buses in July 1986, AEC Routemaster RM1858 (858 DYE) still wears its previous owner's livery but was repainted into corporate colours before entering service in its new home. (Campbell Morrison)

Placed in service by its new owner, Stagecoach, while still wearing the red livery in which it was received from London Buses is AEC Routemaster RM560 (WLT 560), seen here ready to undertake a journey on the former McLennan Perth to Errol service. It is now preserved as part of Stagecoach's heritage fleet. (Author's collection)

Standing at Spittalfield are McLennan's Plaxton-bodied Ford R192 WPT795F, which was new to Trimdon Motor Services in September 1967, and Willowbrook-bodied Ford 570E TOO 557, which began life in August 1962 as a Ford demonstrator. (John Law)

With a Stagecoach board inside the base of its windscreen, and still in the livery of McLennan's, Plaxton-bodied Bedford YRQ SYJ 947L, which started life with Watson, Dundee, in July 1973, is seen here at Spittalfield. (Campbell Morrison)

Seen in Glasgow in heavy snow awaiting its departure to Castlemilk is Magicbus's ex-London AEC Routemaster, WLT 667. (Campbell Morrison)

Still wearing the livery and fleet name of its former owner, Northern General, front-entrance AEC Routemaster RCN 695 is pictured in Glasgow in 1986, soon after its acquisition, followed by Magicbus-liveried ex-London Buses Routemaster 602 DYE. (Author's collection)

Standing outside Magicbus's North Canal Bank Street depot in Glasgow on 9 May 1987 are two front-entrance Routemasters – ex-British Airways NMY 634E and former Northern General FPT 590C. The British Airways example was later fitted with a front destination screen. Still to be seen, it is now part of Ensignbus's heritage fleet.

Leaving Buchanan bus station, Glasgow, on a journey to Easterhouse in January 1987, former Western SMT Alexander-bodied Leyland Leopard SCS 361M carries a Magicbus fleet name and bears the legend 'Hire a Budget Bus' in its destination aperture. (Campbell Morrison)

New to South Yorkshire PTE but still wearing the livery of their former owner Stagecoach Hampshire Bus, Magicbus Van Hool-McArdle-bodied Ailsa B55s LWB 407P and LWB 379P rest between duties at Warroch Street depot, Glasgow, on 7 April 1988.

Standing withdrawn at the Spittalfield graveyard on 6 May 1988 are four ex-Magicbus AEC Routemasters together with Van Hool-McArdle-bodied LWB 380P and NAK 414R, the latter of which still wears the livery of its original owner, South Yorkshire PTE.

Seen in Cotters Warroch Street depot, Glasgow, still wearing its original owner's Coachline livery is Van Hool Alizee-bodied Volvo B10M LJC 800. (Campbell Morrison)

Standing in Warroch Street depot, Glasgow, are AEC Matador recovery wagon JGM 853F, which was acquired from Central SMT and had gained a Magicbus fleet name, and a Magicbus ex-London Buses AEC Routemaster, which is undergoing attention.

Also seen in Magicbus's former Cotters Warroch Street depot, Glasgow, is Neoplan Jetliner 458 5SC wearing Stagecoach corporate colours but carrying a Coachline fleet name. Originally registered A216 LWD, it was new to Maddison, Bilston, in May 1984.

Resting in Buchanan bus station, Glasgow, on 21 August 1989 is Stagecoach Duple-bodied DAF MB230 C895 CSN which displays a Magicbus Londonlink identity for operation on the former Cotters service from Glasgow to London.

Seen while looking down into the yard of Magicbus's Warroch Street depot, Glasgow, on 24 February 1990 are a selection of double-deckers including Bristol Lodekkas, front and rear-entrance Routemasters, ex-Ribble Leyland Atlanteans and a Bristol VRT.

Seen en route to Stanley and wearing Perth Panther Cub fleet names, Robin Hood-bodied Iveco 49.10 033 (G33 PSR) was purchased new in August 1989. (Campbell Morrison)

Caught by the camera at Stagecoach's Inveralmond depot, Perth, on 4 September 1993 is Volvo B58-61 410 (FES 831W), now fitted with a Duple Dominant II body and equipped with fifty-nine bus seats. Being the company's first brand-new coach, it is now preserved by Stagecoach, thus securing its future.

One of a pair of ex-South Yorkshire PTE Leyland-DAB bendibuses purchased from McGill's, Barrhead, in May 1988 for intended use on Magicbus services, FHE 291V is seen here leaving Buchanan bus station, Glasgow, shortly before joining Stagecoach. In the event, however, both buses were immediately transferred to Stagecoach Hampshire Bus without seeing further use in Scotland.

New to McLennan, Spittalfield, in June 1951 with bodywork built by its operator, Leyland PS1 DGS 625 was purchased by Stagecoach from Davies, Pencader, in August 1987 and was restored to its original livery. Now preserved by the company, it is seen here at Spittalfield on 6 May 1988.

Seen in August 1988 at the Spittalfield graveyard (based at the former McLennan premises) are a number of withdrawn Stagecoach buses and several of the Alexander-bodied Leyland Leopards purchased from Kelvin Scottish.

Standing at Spittalfield in one of former McLennan's Nissen huts on 29 August 1988 are three of Stagecoach's recently acquired ex-Kelvin Scottish Alexander-bodied Leyland Leopards – 1749 (GLS 265N), 1753 (GLS 272N) and 1752 (GLS 270N) – of which only 1749/53 were ultimately placed in service by their new owner.

Seen well loaded on its way to Perth in November 1988 is ECW-bodied Bristol VRT HHH 273N, which was borrowed from Stagecoach Cumberland for evaluation, and was later permanently transferred to Scotland.

Still wearing the livery and adverts of its former owner Devon General, recently acquired ECW-bodied Bristol VRT FDV 819V picks up some passengers en route to Perth in January 1989. (Campbell Morrison)

New to West Yorkshire PTE in August 1975, Plaxton-bodied Volvo B58-56 LUB 508P is seen here at the Walnut Grove depot, Perth, of Stagecoach in March 1989 still wearing the livery of Highwayman Coaches from whom it had been purchased a month earlier. (Campbell Morrison)

Adorned in the livery of its former owner Mercers of Longridge, Stagecoach Freight Rover Sherpa D572 EWS (which was new to Badgerline) is seen here in Perth on 26 April 1991 operating a staff shuttle service from the city centre to the Inveralmond depot.

The first of the Leyland Nationals transferred to Perth to be repainted into corporate livery initially for use by Magicbus in Glasgow was former Stagecoach Hampshire Bus GFX 974N which is seen here at Walnut Grove depot, Perth, in April 1989. (S. K. Jenkinson)

Seen at Stagecoach's Perth depot in August 1989 prepared for export to Stagecoach Malawi, ECW-bodied Bristol FLF6G KPW 487E was new to Eastern Counties Omnibus Co. and then served with Eastern Scottish and Kinross Plant before joining Stagecoach in February 1986. After its operation in Malawi it was sold in September 1997 to Adair Investments, also in Malawi. Standing alongside it is Stagecoach Neoplan Skyliner E91 VWA. (Campbell Morrison)

New to Crosville but transferred to Perth from Stagecoach East Midlands, Leyland National 204 (RFM 884M) is seen here on 20 June 1989 wearing Perth Panther branding and operating for free on the first day of the company's onslaught on the city. (Campbell Morrison)

Given Perth Panther fleet names, Stagecoach Plaxton-bodied Volvo B58-61 JSR 42X, which was new in October 1981, rests at its owner's Inveralmond depot, Perth, on 27 October 1989.

Originally registered D614 FSL in April 1987, this Duple 320-bodied Volvo B10M was quickly reregistered D448 FSP and is seen here parked in the yard of Warroch Street depot, Glasgow, on 7 April 1988. (S. A. Jenkinson)

Sister coach D447 FSP, which was originally, albeit briefly, registered D613 FSL, is pictured here at Walnut Grove depot, Perth, in October 1989 shortly after its sale to National Express and transformation into Caledonian Express livery.

Seen in Buchanan bus station, Glasgow, in 1988 is ECW-bodied Bristol FLF6G 083 (GDL 816G). Joining Stagecoach from its original owner, Southern Vectis, in June 1984, it was transferred to Stagecoach's Canadian subsidiary, Gray Coach Lines, Toronto, in January 1992 after being converted to off-side loading.

Although the proposed Tay Tiger fleet name was applied to one of Stagecoach Perth's Leyland Nationals, this was removed before it entered service in Dundee due to it clashing with the identity of a local ice hockey team. (Campbell Morrison)

Adorned with Perth Panther fleet names and passing through Dundee on 27 October 1989 is Stagecoach Perth's only B-series Leyland National, 220 (TRN 811V), which had been transferred from Stagecoach Cumberland in June 1989. (S. K. Jenkinson)

Parked at Alexander Greyhound's Dundee depot on 27 October 1989 is Stagecoach Plaxton-bodied Leyland Leopard RSR 831H, which had been transferred from Stagecoach Cumberland but had begun life with Trent in April 1970 registered ACH 142H. (S. A. Jenkinson)

Seen in Kinnoul Street, Perth, on 26 April 1991 is 362 (FBV 272W), one of a pair of ECW-bodied Bristol LHS6Ls that had arrived in the city from Stagecoach Cumberland in July 1990.

Seen at Stagecoach's Perth depot in January 1992, Bristol FLF6G 082 (KPW 482E) shows its recently fitted off-side door in preparation for its imminent transfer to Stagecoach's Canadian subsidiary, Gray Coach Lines, Toronto. Sold in December 2008 for preservation in Canada, it was resold in March 2011 to Seneca Park Zoo, Rochester, New York, USA, where it is now a static rest room. Standing alongside it is Bristol FLF6G 081 (GDL 769E), which was similarly converted and exported to Gray Coach Lines, but was sadly scrapped in 2004. (Campbell Morrison)

Hired by Stagecoach from Devon General and seen here in its rightful owner's livery operating a Perth local service on 27 October 1989 is Ford Transit 677 (C677 FFJ).

Five of the twenty Ford Transit minibuses hired by Stagecoach from Devon General are seen here at Inveralmond depot, Perth, in December 1989, together with a selection of Stagecoach buses and coaches. (Campbell Morrison)

Stored at Stagecoach's Spittalfield depot between two delicenced Perth Panther Leyland Nationals in March 1990 are former Inverness Traction buses still in their former owner's livery. Alexander-bodied Leyland Leopard L17 (CMS 376L) had been sold by Stagecoach to Inverness Traction in September 1989 and had thus returned home, while Aitken-bodied Freight Rover Sherpa 5 (F212 NST) had been purchased new by Inverness Traction.

Acquired by Stagecoach with the Highwayman Coaches business in February 1989, Whittaker-bodied Mercedes-Benz L608D 250 (A121 XWB) is seen here with Inverness Traction in 1991 wearing an all-over livery for the The Grand Loch Ness Tour. (Campbell Morrison)

New to Scottish Omnibuses in July 1982 registered MSC 556X and later serving with Alexander Northern, Duple-bodied Leyland Tiger 436 (CSU 923) is seen here wearing Stagecoach corporate livery with Inverness Traction identity.

Diverted from Stagecoach Cumberland to Stagecoach Bluebird when brand new in September 1991, corporate-liveried Alexander-bodied Leyland Olympian 090 (J120 XHH) is seen here after its transfer to Stagecoach subsidiary Inverness Traction.

Still wearing Zippy livery but adorned with an Inverness Traction logo on its bonnet, tri-axle Talbot Freeway minibus 42 (E727 UNA) is seen here at Stagecoach's Perth depot awaiting its return to Stagecoach Cumberland after its withdrawal from service at Inverness in January 1990. (Campbell Morrison)

Still displaying its CMS Cumberland fleet names and livery, ECW-bodied Leyland Leopard 635 (RRM 635X) is seen here while on loan to Inverness Traction whose name has been applied below its windscreen. (Campbell Morrison)

New in July 1993, Inverness Traction Alexander-bodied Dennis Dart 514 (K102 XHG) is seen in its home city later that year.

Delicenced at Stagecoach's Spittalfield graveyard are Alexander-bodied Leyland Leopards OSG 553M, which was new to Central SMT, unused former Kelvin Scottish 1752 (GLS 270N), XGM 457L which was latterly used by Magicbus, and AEC Routemaster EDS 247A (originally VLT 43), which had also previously been operated by Magicbus.

Resting in the rain-swept yard of Stagecoach's Warroch Street depot, Glasgow, are Magicbus Bristol FLF6Gs GRX 129D, BHU 976C, DNU 15C and GRX 132D.

Wearing Magicbus fleet names is Alexander-bodied Mercedes-Benz 709D G298 TSL, which was new in March 1990 and is seen here in Glasgow awaiting its departure to Castlemilk. (Campbell Morrison)

New to Crosville in September 1977, Stagecoach ECW-bodied Bristol VRT YTU 358S is seen here at Spittalfield depot on 7 April 1991 fitted with the front panel from United Counties Bristol VRT ANV 776J, which was never operated, having been transferred to Scotland solely for cannibalisation.

Adorned with Perth Panther fleet names, Stagecoach's former Devon General ECW-bodied Bristol VRT 193 (FDV 810V) leaves Inveralmond depot, Perth, in September 1993.

Still wearing its Southdown livery to which Stagecoach names have been added, convertible open-top ECW-bodied Bristol VRT 106 (UWV 608S) stands alongside Bristol FLF6G 071 (BHU 976C) at Inveralmond depot, Perth, in November 1990.

Seen at Inverness Traction's depot adorned with branding for the Inverness–Culloden Tour is Stagecoach-liveried ex-Southdown convertible open-top ECW-bodied Bristol VRT UWV 609S. (Murdoch Currie)

Also branded for the Inverness–Culloden Tour but wearing Guide Friday livery is Stagecoach's ex-Southdown ECW-bodied Bristol VRT, UWV 605S, in open-top format.

New to Greater Manchester PTE, but seen here at Warroch Street depot, Glasgow, on 31 October 1990 after its transfer from Stagecoach Ribble to Magicbus, is NCME-bodied Leyland Atlantean KBU 914P.

Seen in Kinnoul Street, Perth, hiding an Alexander-bodied Mercedes-Benz 709D is Stagecoach's immaculately presented ex-London AEC Routemaster 607 (LDS 201A, originally 607 DYE), both of which are operating on local city services. The Routemaster is now preserved by its owner.

Former London Transport Green Line AEC Routemaster 490 CLT, with rear platform doors, was borrowed for a couple of months by Stagecoach Scotland from Stagecoach Selkent and is seen here alongside ex-Stagecoach Bluebird Alexander-bodied Leyland Leopard 157 (GSO 94V) at Inveralmond depot, Perth, in December 1994. Fortunately, both buses have been privately preserved. (Campbell Morrison)

Hurrying through Easterhouse on its way back to Glasgow on 21 August 1989 when only four months old, Magicbus tri-axle 110-seat Alexander-bodied Leyland Olympian F110 NES carries lettering proclaiming it to be Britain's biggest bus and is now preserved in Stagecoach's heritage collection.

Displaying Stagecoach fleet names, Leyland National 215 (MAO 369P), seen here in Dundee on 21 August 1989, had started life with Cumberland Motor Services in March 1976.

Resting at Aberdeen depot, Alexander-bodied Leyland Olympians NLO62 (C462 SSO) and NLO47 (A47 FRS) respectively display Northern Scottish and Bluebird Northern fleet names on their pre-Stagecoach corporate livery.

Seen at Alexander's factory being converted from dual to single door layout, and still painted in Northern Scottish City Bus livery, are Stagecoach Alexander-bodied Leyland Olympians NLO73–5C (GSO 3–5V) which were originally registered C473–5 SSO. (Campbell Morrison)

Caught by the camera in Aberdeen painted in Stagecoach corporate livery and sporting a Bluebird fleet name, Leyland National 2 PN12 (MSO 12W) began life with Northern Scottish Omnibuses. (Campbell Morrison)

Collecting its Aberdeen-bound passengers in Inverness is Stagecoach Bluebird Van Hool-bodied Volvo B10M 553 (D553 MWR), which was new to Smiths Shearing, Wigan, in February 1987.

New to Magicbus, but seen here in Aberdeen after being transferred to Stagecoach Bluebird Northern, is Alexander-bodied Mercedes-Benz 709D M41 (G289 TSL).

Starting life with Alexander Midland in April 1983 registered BMS 513Y before moving to Kelvin Scottish in 1986, Alexander TE-bodied Leyland Tiger 448 (127 ASV) was acquired by Stagecoach with the Northern Scottish business. Here it is seen at Inverness depot in September 1993, having been repainted in corporate livery with Bluebird Northern fleet names.

Transferred from Stagecoach Hampshire Bus to Stagecoach Bluebird in January 1992, mainly for use on schools services, is rather scruffy ECW-bodied Bristol VRT 128 (RJT1 55R) which later passed to Stagecoach A1 Service in January 1995.

Still wearing its pre-Stagecoach Fife Scottish livery, Leyland National 2 YSX 928W is seen here operating the town service in St Andrews.

Passing Glenrothes bus station on 24 August 1992 is Stagecoach Fife Scottish all-white-liveried Dormobile-bodied Renault S46 46 (E646 DCK), which had been transferred from Stagecoach Ribble. In the background is Stagecoach Fife Scottish ex-Stagecoach Southdown Northern Counties-bodied Volvo Citybus F312 MYJ painted in corporate colours.

Standing in the rain-soaked yard of Dunfermline depot on 30 March 1992 is Stagecoach Fife Scottish's recently repainted, corporate-liveried, Alexander-bodied Leyland Leopard 207 (TMS 407X), which began life with Alexander (Midland).

Leaving Dundee bus station on a journey to its home base at Kirkcaldy on 24 August 1992 is Stagecoach Fife Scottish Alexander-bodied Leyland Tiger 414K (D614 ASG).

Sporting a large Fife Scottish fleet name on its cove panels, Stagecoach corporate-liveried Leyland National 2 YSX 935W is seen here at Stagecoach's Darlington depot en route to Stagecoach Red & White at Chepstow, to where it was being transferred. (Campbell Morrison)

Departing from Dundee bus station at the start of its journey to St Andrews on 24 August 1992 is Stagecoach Fife Scottish Alexander-bodied Ailsa B55 870 (A970 YSX), which was new in March 1984.

Still in pre-Stagecoach livery with BuzzBus branding, Fife Scottish twenty-five-seat MCW Metroriders 66 (F66 RFS) and 67 (F67 RFS) stand in the yard of Kirkcaldy depot on 4 September 1993 beneath the board on the depot wall showing their new owner's name and logo.

Stagecoach in Scotland

About to take up its duties on the St Andrews sightseeing tour on 24 August 1992, Stagecoach Fife Scottish former Southdown open-top ECW-bodied Bristol VRT 605 (UWV 605S) passes through the town's bus station with the depot in the background.

Resting outside the Dunfermline depot of Stagecoach Fife Scottish in August 1992 is the company's tow bus, Leyland Leopard 1051 (XXA 851M), whose Alexander body has been modified for its new role. It started life in April 1974 as a conventional bus with Alexander (Fife).

Parked at Stagecoach's Inveralmond depot, Perth, in August 1991, are two ECW-bodied Leyland Olympians that were new to Alexander (Northern) in spring 1982. On the left, TSO 32X has been repainted into Stagecoach corporate colours and given fleet number 032, while alongside it TSO 16X still wears the livery and fleet number of its former owner (NLO 16M). It will be transformed into corporate colours a few weeks later. (Campbell Morrison)

New to Alexander (Midland) in March 1977, corporate-liveried, Alexander-bodied Leyland Leopard XMS 247R collects its Stirling-bound passengers in East High Street, Crieff, on 9 August 1991.

Seen at Spittalfield depot prepared for one of its several aid trips to Romania, Bristol FLF6G FJB 738C displays a number of fleet names on its staircase panel. New to Thames Valley Traction Co. in November 1965, it had already been converted to a caravan when purchased by Stagecoach in December 1986. Never used in service by its new owner, it was sold in May 1993, and after continuing in use as a caravan in the UK it was exported to Holland in 1996 where it returned to a passenger carrying role before being resold to an operator in Poland in January 2018. (Campbell Morrison)

New to Magicbus in March 1992, and sold a month later to Kelvin Central Buses, Alexander-bodied Dennis Dart J513 FPS was only a few days old when caught by the camera in Glasgow en route to Castlemilk.

Taking their Sunday rest at Magicbus's Hobden Street depot, Glasgow, are several of the company's Routemasters, three Bristol VRTs, a trio of ex-Ribble Leyland Atlanteans and a couple of coaches.

Still wearing the livery of their former owner, four of the five ex-Stagecoach Ribble ECW-bodied Bristol VRTs, including LHG 443T and LHG 442T, stand with two front-entrance Routemasters and a pair of former Ribble NCME-bodied Leyland Atlanteans in the yard of Magicbus's Hobden Street depot, Glasgow, in March 1992. The VRTs had been specifically transferred to Magicbus in preparation for its sale to Kelvin Central Buses.

Pictured on 26 May 1998, with a poster on its side panels promoting the park and ride service in Perth, is Alexander PS-bodied Volvo B10M 594 (M594 OSO) which was new to Bluebird in September 1994.

Promotional advertising for Stagecoach Rail was added to Stagecoach's ex-Fife Scottish Alexander-bodied Leyland Leopard 199 (ASP 352T, originally GSG 133T), seen here at Perth in 1992. (Campbell Morrison)

Travelling through Aberdeen is Norrie's of New Deer's Plaxton-bodied Volvo B58-61 XRP 73S, which began life with York, Cogenhoe, in March 1978. (Author's collection)

New to Alexander (Northern) in November 1978, but later acquired by Western SMT, Stagecoach Western Scottish ECW-bodied Leyland Fleetline FE30AGR KR843 (ASA 23T) is seen at Kilmarnock depot in September 1997 still wearing the livery of its former owner.

Now preserved by Stagecoach and seen here at Ayr depot in September 1997 is Alexander-bodied Leyland PD3A/3 ND1684 (RCS 382) which was new in July 1961 and wears its original Western SMT livery.

New to Kelvin Scottish in August 1986, but seen here in Irvine on 24 March 1995 painted in Western SMT livery, is Stagecoach A1 Service Alexander-bodied Mercedes-Benz L608D D129 NUS.

Approaching Kilmarnock bus station on 24 February 1995 are two Stagecoach Western double-deckers painted in different variations of the old Western Scottish livery. Leading is Park Royal-bodied Leyland Atlantean AN68A/1R KA810 (UNA 824S) which began life with Greater Manchester PTE in August 1977, while behind it is NCME-bodied Leyland Fleetline FE30AGR KR857 (XSJ 657T).

Adorned with 'Strathclyde Transport Dial a Bus' lettering, and still wearing the old livery of Western Scottish, Stagecoach Western's tri-axle Talbot Pullman AT277 (G825 VGA) is seen here in Ayr bus station on 3 September 1994.

Pictured leaving Buchanan bus station, Glasgow, Stagecoach Western Plaxton-bodied Dennis Javelin KN115 (J15 WSB), which was new to Western Scottish in May 1992, is painted in corporate Scottish Citylink livery.

Stored delicenced in Stagecoach Western's Ayr depot on 3 September 1994 are Alexander-bodied Daimler Fleetline CRG6LX HDS 566H, which was new to Alexander (Midland) in February 1970 registered SMS 402H, and ex-Western Scottish NCME-bodied Leyland Fleetline FE30AGR XSJ 656T. Both were new as conventional closed-top buses with the former having latterly operated the Arran open-top tour and the latter maintaining the Ayr sightseeing operation.

Resting at Stagecoach Western's Kilmarnock depot in September 1997 after being relegated to a driver training bus, Alexander-bodied Leyland Leopard W1038 (OSJ 637R) still wears its old Western Scottish livery complete with a Western Engineering fleet name.

Stagecoach Western Scottish Leyland National L701 (UIB 3541), seen here passing through Irvine on 24 February 1995, began life with Central SMT registered EGB 89T.

Seen in September 1997 in the yard of Stagecoach Western Scottish's Kilmarnock depot, unusually carrying a 'Western' fleet name on its Stagecoach corporate livery, Plaxton-bodied Leyland Leopard 628 (TBX1X), which is now preserved, started its life with Leicester City Transport in November 1981.

Lettered for the Arran Open Top Experience, Stagecoach Western Scottish open-top Alexander-bodied Daimler Fleetline CRG6LX 102 (HDS 566H, originally SMS 402H) is seen here in the yard of Ayr depot in September 1997.

Carrying 'Your Wee Happy Bus' branding, Strathclyde Buses MCW Metrorider M89 (E186 BNS), seen here in the yard of its owner's Knightswood depot on 4 September 1994, has since been purchased for preservation and surprisingly restored in Strathtay Scottish livery.

Parked in the yard of Strathclyde Buses' Knightswood depot on 4 September 1994 together with several other Alexander-bodied Leyland Atlanteans are LA1273 (FUS 90T) and LA1208 (XUS 579S).

Passing through central Glasgow in September 1997 on the 45 service to Auchinairn is Strathclyde Buses Alexander-bodied Ailsa B55-10 A119 (B999 YUS).

Painted in Strathclyde Buses SB Travel coaching livery, dual purpose-seated MCW Metrorider GM8 (F238 EDS), which originally carried fleet number M114, is seen here at its owner's Knightswood depot on 4 September 1994.

Following the disastrous fire at Strathclyde Buses' Larkfield depot on 18 May 1992, in which sixty buses were destroyed, the undertaking acquired a number of second-hand buses to provide cover. Among these was former Tyne & Wear PTE, 1976-vintage, Alexander-bodied Leyland Atlantean MVR 512R, which is seen here in Glasgow city centre after being transferred to the company's GCT low cost unit. With its sides painted in Strathclyde orange, it has gained GCT livery on its front and rear.

Another of the fire replacement buses, ex-Nottingham City Transport East Lancs-bodied Leyland Atlantean JAL 879N, which was new in May 1975, is seen here after its transfer to Strathclyde Buses' low cost GCT unit, in whose livery it is seen here in central Glasgow in 1994, numbered GLA10.

Purchased new by Stagecoach Glasgow in November 1994 in preparation for the company's re-entry into the city, Alexander PS-bodied Volvo B10M M778 PRS was, along with its sisters, sold to Strathclyde Buses' KCB Network subsidiary before its entry into service with its intended operator. Here it is seen still in Stagecoach's striped livery but with its front repainted into KCB red. (Campbell Morrison)

Standing in the yard of Stagecoach's Inveralmond depot, Perth, are ex-Barrow Transport East Lancs-bodied Dodge S56 (D456 BEO, which for the first twelve months of its life was registered D459 BEO), and Alexander-bodied Mercedes-Benz 709D 312 (G201 PAO), which had been purchased new in May 1990. After spending a brief time with Stagecoach subsidiary Inverness Traction, 351 (D456 BEO) was largely used as a staff rest room at Mill Street, Perth. (Campbell Morrison)

Seen in Perth operating a city service in April 1992 is Stagecoach ECW-bodied Bristol VRT 097 (JNU 134N). Transferred from Stagecoach East Midlands to Magicbus in April 1990, by 2012 it had found a new home in Tenerife, where it is incorporated into a crazy golf course.

Standing at Parkhouse bus station, Ardrossan, on 24 February 1995, still in the livery of A1 Service but with the addition of Stagecoach A1 Service fleet names and fleet number 906, Roe-bodied Leyland Olympian EWY 76Y began life on lease to West Yorkshire PTE in March 1983.

Three different liveries are to be seen here at Parkhouse bus station, Ardrossan, on 24 February 1995. Still in A1 Service colours is Wright Endurance-bodied Volvo B10B M151 FGB, which was new to Docherty, Irvine, in November 1994 registered M1 ABO, while next to it, still in Western SMT livery, is an Alexander-bodied Seddon Pennine VII with a former Stagecoach London Leyland Titan, still in its previous owner's colour, in the background. M151 FGB is now preserved by its original A1 Service owner.

Resting in the yard of Stagecoach's Ardrossan depot on 24 February 1995 are a selection of former A1 Service buses still in their original owner's livery. Interloper ex-Stagecoach Western Scottish AA801 (UNA 863S), a former Greater Manchester PTE Park Royal-bodied Leyland Atlantean, is flanked by Alexander-bodied Ailsa B55-10 951 (NSP 331R), which had begun life with Tayside, and Roe-bodied Leyland Atlantean AN68B/1R 818 (HSJ 61V) which had been purchased new by A1 member A. Hunter.

Seen in Stagecoach's Ardrossan depot yard in February 1995 are ECW-bodied Leyland Olympian 023 (TSO 23X), which had been transferred from Stagecoach Perth, and former Volvo demonstrator A308 RSU, an East Lancs-bodied Volvo B10M-50 Citybus still in A1 Service livery, albeit with Stagecoach A1 Service fleet names.

Still wearing the livery of its former owner, Stagecoach London, and using a temporary destination display, Stagecoach A1 Service Leyland Titan OHV 684Y, which has since been preserved, approaches Kilmarnock bus station on 25 February 1995.

Repainted into corporate livery but still retaining its dual-door layout, Stagecoach A1 Service's ex-Stagecoach London Leyland Titan GYE 273W is seen here at Parkhouse bus station, Ardrossan, on 24 February 1995.

Displaying Stagecoach A1 Service fleet names, ECW-bodied Bristol VRT 826 (RJT 155R) passes through Irvine on 24 February 1995. New to Hants & Dorset in April 1983, it was transferred to Stagecoach Bluebird in January 1992 before moving to Stagecoach A1 Service in January 1995.

New to Stagecoach A1 Service in August 1995, Alexander-bodied Volvo Olympian 927 (N861 VHH) is seen here in Irvine in September 1997 in Stagecoach corporate livery.

Starting life with Southdown in May 1986, PMT-bodied Mercedes-Benz L608D 234 (C591 SHC), with Stagecoach A1 Service fleet names, stands in Ardrossan depot while being used on staff shuttle duties in February 1995.

Despite displaying a school bus sign on its radiator grill, Stagecoach A1 Service's ex-Clyde Coast Services Dormobile-bodied Mercedes-Benz 709D 266 (L961 UGA) heads through Irvine on route 27 to Heatherstane in September 1997.

Four ex-Stagecoach London Leyland Titans and a former Western Scottish Daimler Fleetline stand in the yard of Stagecoach's Kilmarnock depot in 1997. The Titans were all being cannibalised for spares to keep their sisters running.

New in September 1994, Stagecoach Western Scottish East Lancs-bodied Volvo B10M SV431 (WGB 646W) reverses off the stand in Ayr bus station at the start of its long journey to Stranraer in September 1997.

New to Western SMT in June 1981 registered NCS 121W and fitted with Duple Dominant IV coachwork, 431 (VLT 154) was given a new East Lancs body in 1994. Now owned by Stagecoach Western Scottish, it is seen here in Ayr bus station in September 1997 branded for the long 585 ClydeCoaster service, which was operated jointly with Clyde Coast Services and AA Buses.

Immaculately presented and standing in the yard of Stagecoach's Inveralmond depot, Perth, is Plaxton coach-bodied Volvo B10M 561 (K561 GSA), which was purchased new in February 1993.

Leaving Buchanan bus station, Glasgow, on the X25 express service to Abronhill in September 1997 is Stagecoach Fife's Jonckheere-bodied Volvo B10M bendi-coach 562 (N562 SJF), which was purchased new in June 1996.

Displaying a Stagecoach Glasgow fleet name and Lo-Liner branding, Alexander-bodied Volvo B6LE 366 (P366 DSA) is seen here leaving Buchanan bus station, Glasgow, on 4 September 1997.

Also leaving Buchanan bus station, Glasgow, in September 1997 on the 4A service to Newton Mearns is Stagecoach Western Scottish ex-Stagecoach London Leyland Titan 938 (WYV 27T), which still retains its dual-door layout.

Both new to AA member Young of Ayr, but now under Stagecoach ownership despite retaining AA Buses livery, Leyland National 2 761 (FSD 687V) and Leyland National 708 (YSJ 14T) stand in the yard of Stagecoach's Ayr depot in September 1997.

New to AA member Dodds of Ayr in September 1995, Alexander (Belfast)-bodied Mercedes-Benz 709D 063 (N586 WND), now under Stagecoach ownership, rests at its new owner's Ayr depot in September 1997.

Still wearing the AA Buses livery of Dodds of Ayr, by whom it was purchased new in March 1995, Northern Counties-bodied Dennis Dart 403 (M388 KVR) prepares to leave the Ayr depot of its new owner, Stagecoach Western Scottish, in September 1997.

New as N607 WND but re-registered P741 HND, Stagecoach Western Scottish Plaxton-bodied Dennis Dart SLF 409 was new to Dodds of Ayr in August 1996 and still wears AA Buses identity in its side windows as it passes through Irvine in September 1997.

Inherited with Stagecoach's purchase of AA Buses was 1956-vintage Burlingham Seagull-bodied Guy Warrior SJW 515, which is seen here on 26 May 1998 after being repainted into Bluebird livery for use on heritage tours of Perthshire.

Open-top Park Royal-bodied Daimler CRL6 104 (GHV 102N) started life as a conventional closed-top London Transport double-decker in June 1975. Acquired by Stagecoach Selkent in 1994 it was transferred to Stagecoach Western Scottish in August 1995 and is seen here at Ayr depot in September 1997, branded for the Burns Heritage Tour. Sold in 1999, it then found a new home in Toronto, Canada.

New to Alder Valley registered B577 LPE, but acquired by Stagecoach Western Scottish from Cleveland Transit and seen here in Ayr in September 1997, ECW-bodied Leyland Olympian 911 (PJI 4983) is pictured wearing an all-over advert for Butlin's Wonderwest holiday camp at Ayr.

During the 1990s Stagecoach purchased a large number of Alexander PS-bodied Volvo B10Ms for its various subsidiaries, one of which – three month-old Western Scottish's KV593 (M793 PRS) – is seen in Kilmarnock in February 1995.

Entering Ayr bus station in September 1997 is Stagecoach Western Scottish former Stagecoach London Leyland Titan 935 (CUL 179V) which wears an all-over advert for Butlin's Wonderworld, thus promoting the service on which it is operating.

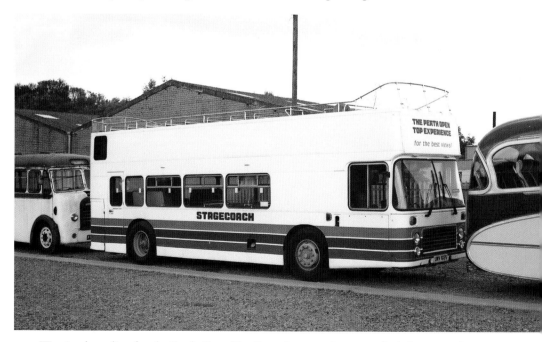

Wearing branding for the Perth Open Top Experience on its upper-deck front panel, open-top former Stagecoach East Kent ECW-bodied Bristol VRT 075 (UWV 613S), which began life with Southdown, is seen delicenced at its owner's Inveralmond depot, Perth, on 26 May 1998. Ten years later, refitted with its roof, it was exported to start a new life in Spain.

Starting life with Stagecoach Inverness Traction in September 1993, Northern Counties-bodied Volvo Olympian 101 (L101 JSA) was later transferred to Perth, where it is seen here in 1995. (Campbell Morrison)

Low-height ECW-bodied Bristol VRT RPR 716R was transferred from Stagecoach Hampshire Bus to Scotland in January 1992 and numbered 084, before moving from Inverness Traction to Stagecoach Fife (who renumbered it 1128) in September 1994. Standing alongside it at Cowdenbeath depot in April 1996 are full-height ECW-bodied Bristol VRTs 1120/1 (DWF 198/9V) which were acquired by Stagecoach Fife Scottish from Stagecoach East Midlands in August 1994. As can be seen, all three buses were mainly used on school services.

One of four Willowbrook-bodied Bristol VRTs transferred in July 1994 from Stagecoach East Kent to Stagecoach Fife Scottish for school bus duties, 1126 (TFN 990T) is seen here at Cowdenbeath depot in September 1997.

Transferred from Stagecoach Selkent to Stagecoach Fife Scottish in December 1996, Leyland Titans 762 (OHV 801Y) and 760 (KYV 455X) were both converted from dual to single-door layout before entering service in their new Scottish home.

Stagecoach A1 Service Alexander-bodied Volvo Olympian 922 (N856 VHH) is seen in Irvine in 1998 after being repainted into the old A1 livery.

New to Stringfellow, Fleetwood, in November 1988, Plaxton-bodied DAF MB230 472 (F637 OHD) later served with Stagecoach Selkent before migrating north to Perth, where it is seen here in 1995. (Campbell Morrison)

New to Stagecoach Ribble in August 1996, Stagecoach Fife Scottish Plaxton-bodied Volvo B10MA bendi-coach 573 (P573 UBV) leaves Buchanan bus station, Glasgow, in September 1997 on the X15 express service to Dunfermline.

Starting life with Stagecoach Bluebird in September 1995, Plaxton-bodied Volvo B10M 618 (N618 USS) is seen here wearing National Express corporate livery. (Author's collection)

Collecting its passengers in Perth on 26 September 1998 is Stagecoach Alexander-bodied Leyland Olympian C469 SSO which began life with Northern Scottish in July 1986.

Seen in Mill Street, Perth, while operating various city services are Alexander-bodied Volvo B6LE P496 BRS adorned with 'New Super Low Floor Easy Access Bus' lettering on its cove panels, and two Alexander PS-bodied Volvo B10Ms headed by 573 (K573 LTS).

A busy scene in Mill Street, Perth, in 1996 shows Stagecoach's ex-Northern Scottish ECW-bodied Leyland Olympian 030 (TSO 30X) along with one of its sisters, an Alexander-bodied Leyland Leopard, two Routemasters and an independent operator's coach.

Transferred from Stagecoach Selkent to Scotland in November 1997 and converted to open-top configuration, Leyland Titan 084 (B114 WUV) overtakes Alexander-bodied Volvo B6LE 496 (P496 BRS) in Perth as it operates the city's sightseeing tour in May 1998.